## Help with timing

★ As the Science National Test papers are timed, it is important that your child learns to answer questions within a time limit.

★ Each *Test yourself* section and each *National Test Questions* section gives target times for answering the questions. If you choose to, you can ask your child to time himself/herself when answering the questions. You can then compare his/her time against the target times provided in the *Answers and Guidance*. In this way, you will form a good idea of whether your child is working at the right rate to complete the Science National Test papers successfully.

## Progression

★ *Success in Science* is aimed at 9–11 year-olds who are in Years 5 and 6 of primary school. Books 1 and 2 cover topics that children are normally taught in school in Year 5 (ages 9/10). Books 3 and 4 cover topics that children are normally taught in school in Year 6 (ages 10/11).

★ To get the most out of *Success in Science*, it is important that your child works through all four books in sequence. If you are buying this series for your child who is already in Year 6, then it is still advisable to work through from Book 1 to Book 4, to ensure that your child benefits from the progression built into the series.

## Note to teachers

★ This book, and the other three titles in the *Success in Science* series, are designed for use at home and in schools in Years 5 and 6. They focus on the key science concepts and skills that will raise children's performance in the Science National Test.

★ You can use the books in class or give them to children for homework to ensure that they are fully prepared for their Science National Test.

# 1 Your skeleton and teeth

**What you need to know**

⭐ Why do we need a skeleton?

⭐ What are joints?

⭐ What are muscles?

⭐ Why do we have different types of teeth?

⭐ What should we do to look after our teeth?

This chapter will help you to answer these key questions.

## Your skeleton

All the bones in your body are called your **skeleton**. The diagram shows many of the larger bones in your skeleton. You do not need to know the names of all the bones in your body, but it is useful to know some of the larger ones.

Did you know there are over 200 bones in your body? The smallest bones are inside your ear.

The skeleton has three main jobs:

- **to support your body**
- **to help you to move**
- **to protect parts of your body**

Without a skeleton you would not be able to support your body. You would be floppy and would not be able to stand up straight.

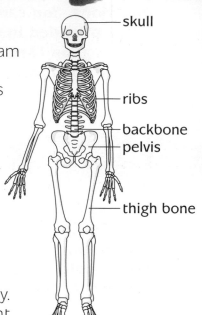

skull

ribs

backbone

pelvis

thigh bone

You also need your skeleton to be able to move. Your muscles are attached to your bones and together the muscles and bones work to allow you to walk, run and jump.

Some parts of the skeleton protect parts of your body from damage. The **skull** protects your brain and the **ribs** protect your heart and lungs.

## Your joints

We call the place where two or more bones are joined together a **joint**. There are two main types of joint that allow your body to move in different ways.

One type of joint is called a **hinge joint**. Your knee is an example of a hinge joint. Bend your knee and move your foot forwards and back. The joint behind your knee cap allows you to move your lower leg and foot forward and back. It does not allow you to move your lower leg from side to side.

Another type of joint is called a **ball and socket joint**. Your shoulder joint is an example of a ball and socket joint. Swing your arm around. You can move it in most directions. The ball and socket joint allows your arm to move from side to side as well as forwards and back.

## Your muscles

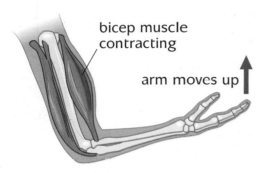

bicep muscle contracting

arm moves up↑

**Muscles** are attached to your bones and help you to move. Muscles work by getting shorter; we say the muscle **contracts**. As muscles contract, they pull on the bone they are attached to. The diagram shows what happens when the bicep muscle in your arm contracts. The muscle is attached to a bone in the lower arm, and when it contracts the lower arm raises. If you put your hand on the top of your arm and move your lower arm up and down you will feel the muscle working.

## Your teeth

**Teeth** are part of your skeleton. They are fixed into the jaw bone. As a child you have 28 teeth that eventually fall out and are replaced by 32 adult teeth. Your 28 first teeth are called **milk teeth**.

Our teeth are very important. We use them to bite and chew a range of food, breaking the food down into little bits that we can swallow.

## Different types of teeth

If you look carefully at your teeth in a mirror you will be able to see that there are different shaped teeth. Each type of tooth has a different job.

**Incisors** are at the front of your mouth and are designed for cutting food. They are sharp with a straight edge. Imagine biting into an apple. The incisors cut off the first piece of apple you want to eat.

incisors have a sharp cutting surface

**Molars** are at the back of your mouth and are used for crushing and grinding food. They have a large surface and are shaped with ridges so that the top and bottom teeth can grind against each other when you chew food.

molars have a flat, ridged crushing/grinding surface

There is a pair of **canines** on both your top and lower jaw. Each canine tooth is positioned between the incisors and the molars, one each side. Canines are used to tear food, particularly tough food such as meat. Canine teeth are sharp and pointed.

canines have a rounded point for holding and tearing

# Looking after your teeth

It is very important to look after your teeth carefully. They have to last you a lifetime!

Your teeth need to be brushed at least twice a day. This brushing is important to stop the build up of bacteria on your teeth. The bacteria break down sugar to form acid. The acid decays your teeth. The sticky layer of bacteria on your teeth is called **plaque**.

Eating less sugary food between meals will help reduce the amount of plaque that develops.

A regular visit to the dentist is important to keep your teeth in really good condition. The dentist can spot early signs of decay and help you look after your teeth so that you do not need to have fillings.

## Using your knowledge

### Do all children have the same number of each type of tooth?

Some children decided to investigate whether they had the same number of each type of tooth. They used some special plastic to make an imprint of their teeth. Each child bit down hard onto a soft plastic sheet and their teeth made marks. The diagrams show the marks made by their teeth from their top jaw.

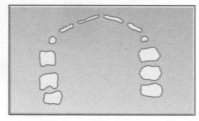

*Rachel's teeth*

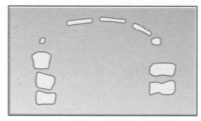

*Tim's teeth*

● Can you work out which mark is left by which type of tooth?

The molars have a large surface area and look square from above. The large surface is needed for grinding food up.

Each incisor has a thin, straight biting edge, used for cutting into food.

The canine leaves a rounded pointed mark. This type of tooth is pointed because it is used to grip and tear food.

The children compared their jaw imprints.

● Do the two children have the same number of each type of tooth?

Tim has one less incisor than Rachel, and one less molar. He has not grown all of his second teeth yet, so the gaps left by the milk teeth he has lost are shown as gaps on the tooth imprint.

1 Which part of the skeleton protects your brain?

2 Name three jobs that the skeleton does.

3 **a** What type of joint is your elbow?

 **b** What type of joint is your hip?

4 Our teeth have different roles, helping us to eat our food. Match up the type of tooth with its special job.

canine

cuts food

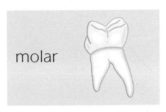
molar

tears food

incisor

grinds food

5 List three ways to help care for your teeth.

6 Explain why it is important not to have sugar on your teeth for a long period of time.

7 Look again at *Using your knowledge*. You have found out that molars have a large surface that allows these teeth to grind up food easily. How else are the molars adapted to help grind up food?

Answers and Guidance are given on p.41. | **How long did you take?**

# 2 Your heart and blood

**What you need to know**

★ What does the heart do?

★ How does blood move around the body?

★ What does your pulse measure?

★ What happens to your pulse during and after exercise?

★ How can you keep your heart healthy?

This chapter will help you to answer these key questions.

## Your heart

The **heart** is a very important organ in your body. It is positioned in your chest, slightly to the left-hand side. If you clench your fist, that is about the size of your heart. The role of the heart is to pump blood around the body.

In Chapter 1 we found out that muscles work by contracting. When the muscle of the heart contracts, it squeezes blood out of the heart and around the body through blood vessels. When the heart relaxes, blood drains into the heart from the body through other blood vessels. Each contraction of the heart is a **heart beat**.

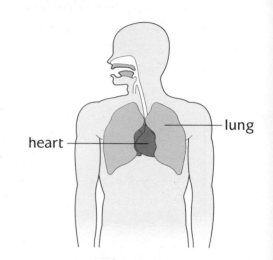

## Blood vessels

The blood leaves the heart, and moves away from the heart, in blood vessels called **arteries**. (A vessel is a tube.) The blood returns to the heart in vessels called **veins**.

Arteries and veins are the largest types of blood vessels in the body. **Capillaries** join arteries to veins.

## Pulse rate

Every person and lots of animals have a **pulse**. You can feel your pulse in your neck and in your wrist.

When you feel your pulse, you are actually feeling the flow of blood as the heart contracts and pushes more blood around the body. These pushes can be counted. Your **pulse rate** is a measure of how fast your heart is beating. We also call this the **heart beat rate**. Normally your pulse rate is given as the number of beats per minute.

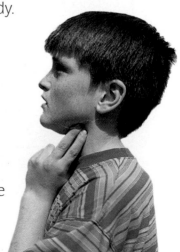

| | Pulse rate (heart beats per minute) |
|---|---|
| Adult | 70 |
| Child | 85 |

The average pulse rate for an adult is around 70 beats per minute. A child's heart beats quicker, around 85 beats per minute.

## Pulse rate and exercise

Exercise makes your heart beat more quickly. If your body is working harder to run, swim or do some other exercise, your muscles need more food and oxygen to keep them working.

Food and oxygen are carried to the muscles in the blood. If the muscles are working harder, then the heart also has to work harder by beating faster to send more blood containing food and oxygen to the muscles.

Once you stop exercising your muscles recover and need less food and oxygen. Your heart does not need to send the blood around the body so quickly so the heart beat rate slows down. Eventually it drops to its normal **resting** heart beat rate. We can also call this the **resting pulse rate**.

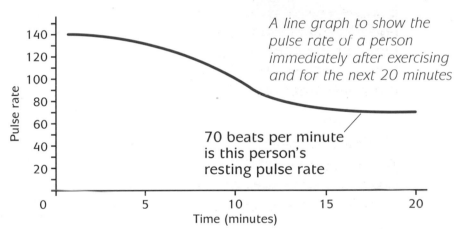

70 beats per minute is this person's resting pulse rate

*A line graph to show the pulse rate of a person immediately after exercising and for the next 20 minutes*

## Keeping your heart healthy

It is very important to keep your heart healthy. You can help to look after your heart by following some golden rules:

- do not smoke
- eat a balanced diet without too much fatty food
- take regular exercise

Jump Rope For Heart

*'Jump Rope for Heart' is the British Heart Foundation's popular sponsored skipping scheme that raises money both for the heart charity and your school or group.*

### What happens to your heart beat rate during and after exercise?

As part of a project on healthy living, some children decided to find out what happened to their heart beat rate after exercise.

Three children measured their pulse rate before exercising, immediately after 5 minutes of exercise and then 5 minutes later.

The bar chart shows their results.

- What pattern do the results from all three children show?

For each of the children, their pulse rate increased dramatically during exercise. After 5 minutes of rest, the pulse rate of all three children had started to drop.

- What pulse rate would you expect Matthew to have after a further 20 minutes of rest?

Matthew's pulse rate should drop back to his original measurement of 80 beats per minute after 20 minutes of rest. This is his resting pulse rate.

Susan also did the same investigation but she measured her pulse rate before exercise and then every minute after exercise for 12 minutes.

- How could she show her results on a graph?

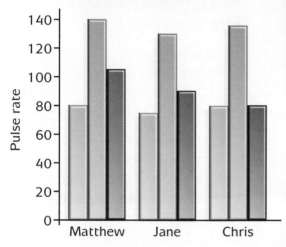

*A bar chart to show the pulse rate of three children*

pulse rate before exercise

pulse rate immediately after exercise

pulse rate 5 minutes after exercise

Susan would be best drawing a line graph as she has a lot of data recorded in little steps.
The line graph can be used as a record for all the data and any patterns can be seen easily. This graph shows that Susan's pulse rate fell to 86 in the 12 minutes of rest following exercise. Her pulse rate before exercise was 80 beats per minute.

We will look again at presenting and using results like these in Chapter 6 of Book 4.

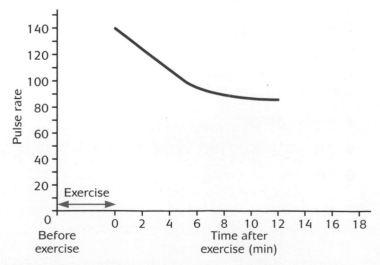

*A line graph to show Susan's pulse rate for 12 minutes after exercise*

**1** What is the job of the heart?

**2** Which part of the skeleton protects the heart?

**3** Fill in the gaps in the passage below.

Blood moves away from the heart in blood vessels called ................................................................. .

It returns to the heart in blood vessels called

................................................................. .

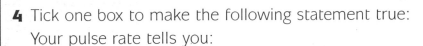

**4** Tick one box to make the following statement true:

Your pulse rate tells you:

☐ how many times you breathe in, in a minute

☐ how many times you breathe in and out in a minute

☐ how many times your heart beats in a minute

☐ the amount of blood being pumped around your body

☐ your blood pressure

**5** Explain why your heart beat rate goes up when you do exercise.

**6** What happens to your pulse rate when you stop exercising?

**7** Look again at the results of the investigation by Susan in *Using your knowledge*. Can you use the graph to estimate when Susan's pulse rate will return to its resting rate?

Answers and Guidance are given on p.41.    ***How long did you take?***

🕐 *You should be able to complete these questions in 12 minutes*

**1** **(a)** The dentist gave this child a tablet which dyes the plaque on the teeth.

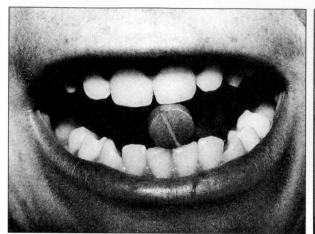 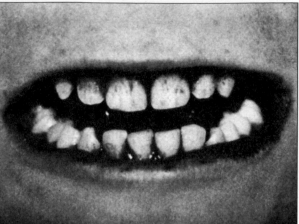

Before using coloured dye          After using coloured dye

Plaque leads to tooth decay.

> What can you do to stop plaque building up on your teeth between visits to the dentist?

..................................................................................................................................................

*1 mark*

**(b)** Different types of tooth do different jobs when we bite food.

Look at the picture.

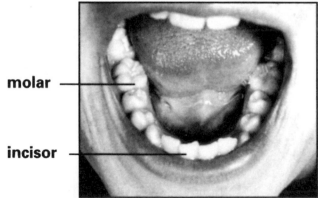

molar ——
incisor ——

> What **different** jobs do these two types of tooth do?

molar..................................................................................................................................

incisor................................................................................................................................

*2 marks*

1998 A1

12

2

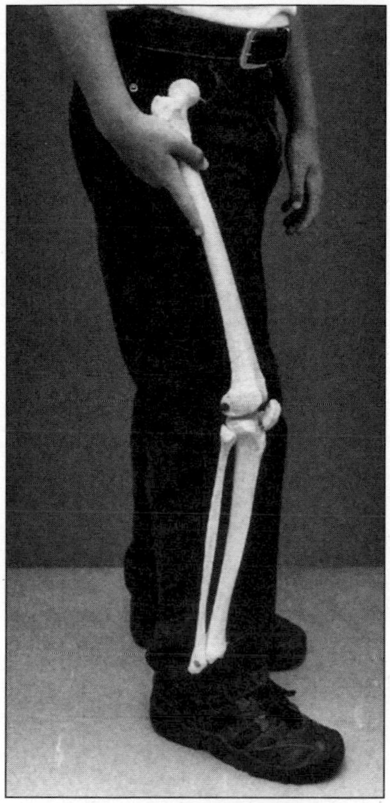

(a) Dan is thinking about what his muscles and bones do.

> What must his leg muscles do to raise his foot?

Tick **ONE** box.

☐ expand      ☐ twist

☐ contract    ☐ push

*1 mark*

(b) Write **TWO** different ways in which having a skeleton is important to humans.

(i).....................................................................................................
*1 mark*

(ii)....................................................................................................
*1 mark*

1996 A10

**3** **(a)** Which of these **could** lead to a greater chance of heart disease?

Tick **TWO** boxes.

☐ regular exercise

☐ smoking

☐ eating lots of fruit and vegetables

☐ eating lots of fatty foods

☐ not washing regularly

*2 marks*

**(b)** Two children studied a model of a human heart.

What does the heart do to the blood inside the body?

.............................................................................................................

*1 mark*

**(c)** What is the name of the blood vessels which carry blood **to** the heart?

..........................................................................................................

*1 mark*

**(d)** Mary took part in three activities.

She measured her heart beat rate just after each activity.

She measured the rate again after resting for 30 minutes.

She recorded her results.

Complete the table to show her heart beat rate after resting for 30 minutes.

| **Activity** | **Heart beat rate in beats per minute** | |
|---|---|---|
| | **just after activity** | **after resting for 30 minutes** |
| writing | 79 | 78 |
| walking | 117 | ...................... |
| running | 173 | ...................... |

*1 mark*

**(e)** Explain how you decided what heart beat rates to write in the table.

..........................................................................................................

*1 mark*

1997 A6

Answers and Guidance are given on p.45. ***How long did you take?***

**What you need to know**

★ What is a solid, liquid and gas?

★ What do all solids have in common?

★ What do all liquids have in common?

★ What do all gases have in common?

★ What are the scientific names for the changes of state?

This chapter will help you to answer these key questions.

## Solids, liquids and gases

A substance is usually a **solid**, or a **liquid** or a **gas**. Solid, liquid and gas are **states** a substance can be in.

| Solids | Liquids | Gases |
|---|---|---|
| Examples: | Examples: | Examples: |
| Bread | Orange juice | Fizzy bubbles in lemonade |
| Book | Milk | Balloon (air) |
| Key | Water | Car exhaust fumes |

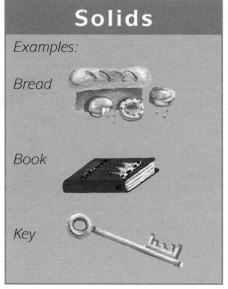

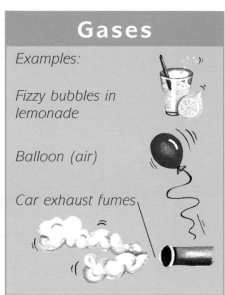

## Solids

All solids have some properties in common.

- Solids can all be 'got hold of'.
  You cannot pick up liquids and gases.

- A solid holds its own shape
  when you leave it alone.

- Solids can be cut or shaped.

- Most solids cannot be poured.

Some solids, such as sugar and sand, are made of very small particles. If a lot of the small particles are together, it may seem that the substance flows and that you cannot pick it up. For example, sand will flow through your fingers if you try to pick it up. But each tiny piece of sand holds its shape and cannot flow.

## Liquids

All liquids have some properties in common.

- Liquids are runny and can be poured.
- Liquids will take the shape of the container they are poured into.
- Liquids will always spread out to the lowest level they can. You will never see a mound of liquid!
- The surface of a liquid stays level if you tip the container.

*These spilt liquids are spreading out as much as possible.*

Some liquids, such as honey and thick oil, do not seem to be runny. They **are** runny, but they take a long time to move. They will move (run) more quickly if they are heated.

## Gases

All gases have some properties in common.

- Gases are not always easy to see; many are invisible.
- You cannot hold a gas.
- A gas tries to spread out as much as possible.
- A gas will fill the shape of the container it is in.

Air freshener sprays work because the gas tries to spread out as much as possible. The gas is put into the can under pressure. As soon as the gas is released by pressing the button on the can, the perfumed gas spreads itself throughout the room.

Remember that we have a mixture of gases all around us all of the time: air. Air is made up of several gases, including oxygen. We need oxygen to stay alive.

## The scientific names for changes of state

We can change the state of some substances by heating them or cooling them down. These changes have scientific names.

If a solid turns into a liquid we say it has **melted**. The solid needs to get warmer for melting happen.

If a liquid turns into a solid we say it has **frozen**. The liquid needs to get colder for freezing happen.

Solid ice cream

Melting

Freezing

Liquid ice cream

If a liquid changes into a gas we say it has **evaporated**. If a liquid is warmed it will evaporate more quickly.

If a gas changes into a liquid we say it has **condensed**. If a gas gets colder it will condense.

The substance that is changing from a liquid to a solid or gas and back again is still the same substance, it is just in different states.

In Book 2 we will look more closely at the different states of water.

Evaporation →

Condensation ←

evaporation

Water from the hot tea evaporates as water vapour

Water vapour in the air condenses into water on the cold glass

condensation

## Using your knowledge

### Can you compress or squash a solid, liquid or gas?

Some children decided to find out for themselves whether you can compress solids, liquids and gases. They decided to investigate using orange juice (liquid), sand (solid) and air (gas).

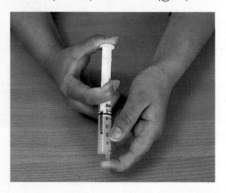

They put $5\,cm^3$ of orange juice into a syringe, $5\,cm^3$ of sand into a syringe and $5\,cm^3$ of air into a syringe. Then they sealed the nozzle end of each syringe with their fingers and pushed to the plunger to see if they could compress the substance.

They made a table of their results.

| Substance | Reading on syringe after compression |
|---|---|
| | $5\,cm^3$ |
| | $0.5\,cm^3$ |
| | $5\,cm^3$ |

● Can you guess which substance gave which reading?

Only the air (gas) could be compressed: it squashed to $0.5\,cm^3$. The orange juice (liquid) and the sand (solid) did not squash and remained at $5\,cm^3$.

One of the boys got an air bubble in his syringe when he filled it with orange juice.

● Can you describe what happened when he tried to compress his syringe?

It seemed as though the liquid could be compressed a little because the plunger would move slightly. What was really happening was that the air bubble (gas) was being squashed, not the orange juice (liquid).

air in balloon

deckchair

lemonade bottle

bubbles in lemonade

suntan lotion

sand

sea

plastic bucket

sea shell

**1** Put the labelled substances from the beach into three sets: solid, liquid and gas.

**2** If you take a packet of butter out of the fridge it is a hard solid. Give two properties of a solid that apply to the butter.

**3** As you heat butter in a pan it turns to liquid. What two properties does the liquid now have that the solid butter did not?

**4** Name one property that gases have that liquids do **not** have.

**5** Label each arrow with the correct scientific word to describe the change of state.

**a** Solid ⟶ Liquid

**b** Gas ⟶ Liquid

**c** Liquid ⟶ Gas

**6** What property do sand and sugar appear to have that is different to most solids? Why do they have this property?

**7** Look again at *Using your knowledge*. The children decided to test some more substances: iron filings, water, plasticine and fizzy lemonade. Can you complete their results table?

| Substance | Reading on syringe after compression |
|---|---|
| *Sand* | $5\,cm^3$ |
| *Air* | $0.5\,cm^3$ |
| *Orange juice* | $5\,cm^3$ |
| | $5\,cm^3$ |
| | $4.8\,cm^3$ |
| | $5\,cm^3$ |
| *Plasticine* | |

Answers and Guidance are given on p.42.  *How long did you take?*

## Changing state

In Chapter 3 we found out that substances are usually a solid, liquid or gas and we called this the **state of the substance**. Substances can change from one state into another. You can change the state of a substance by heating or cooling it. For example, water can change between the states of solid, liquid or gas if it is heated or cooled.

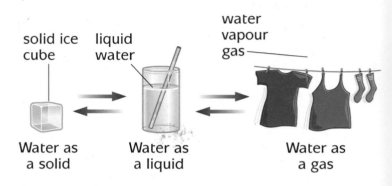

solid ice cube   liquid water   water vapour gas

Water as a solid    Water as a liquid    Water as a gas

cooling

## Cooling and heating

The most common example of a change of state because of cooling is when something is **frozen**. A freezer has a temperature of about −8°C, well below the freezing point of water. When liquid water is put in the freezer it changes state and turns from a liquid into a solid.

When the ice (solid water) is taken out of the freezer and allowed to warm up to the temperature of the room, it turns back into a liquid (water).

If you melt chocolate, it turns from a solid into a liquid, but it is still chocolate. It will change back into solid chocolate on cooling. Margarine is another example of a solid that will melt on heating but change back to a solid when it is allowed to cool.

Some liquids, like water, can be heated and turned into a gas (water vapour) and will then turn back into a liquid when cooled. For example, when water vapour condenses against a cold window pane it turns back into water droplets.

## Reversible changes

The changes of state we have found out about so far are all **reversible changes**. This means that if the substance is given the opposite treatment it can be changed back into its original form. The substance is always the same, it is only the state, whether it is a solid, liquid or gas, that has changed. We call these changes **physical changes** because the changes have only been to the physical properties of the substance.

## Irreversible changes

Sometimes when substances are heated they change and cannot be changed back into their original form. Think about frying an egg. The egg changes from being a runny liquid to a solid once it is cooked. You cannot change it back again. Once it has been cooked it is always cooked and will stay a solid. This change is an **irreversible change**.

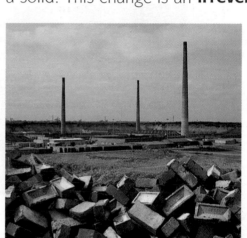

Irreversible changes are permanent. This can be very useful. Building bricks are made out of clay. The clay is heated at very high temperatures in a special oven called a kiln. The clay changes to form a different solid that we call brick. The original clay can soften in water, but the cooked clay, which is a different substance, does not. The bricks cannot be changed back to the original clay, and our brick houses will not crumble in rain!

In all the examples of irreversible changes new substances have been made. A new substance means new chemicals have been made. This means irreversible changes are caused by **chemical changes**.

## Burning

When something **burns**, heat is given out and the original substance is changed permanently. So a change caused by burning is an irreversible, chemical change. Burning is different to heating. Burning involves a chemical reaction, heating and melting do not.

Think about wood burning on a fire. The wood burns and ends up as a pile of ash. This ash cannot be turned back into wood.

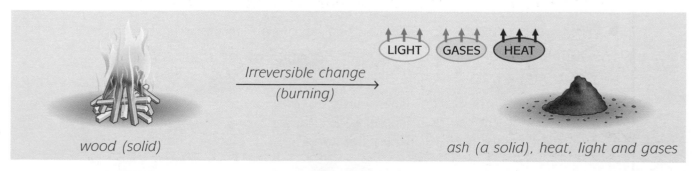

wood (solid)

*Irreversible change (burning)*

LIGHT  GASES  HEAT

ash (a solid), heat, light and gases

*Irreversible change*
*(burning)*

*Wax (solid)*

*Heat, light and gases*

Some of the wax of a lit candle will melt because of the heat caused by the burning wick and candle. If the candle is not in a container then the melted wax, which is liquid, will flow away and not burn. A night light is in a container so the liquid wax cannot flow away from the wick and eventually all the wax will burn. This is why night lights last much longer than tall candles. Remember, melting is a reversible reaction but burning is not.

# Using your knowledge

### The 'changes' game

A group of children have made up a game about changes. The winner is the first person to match each of the picture cards showing a change with the correct type of change: whether it is reversible or irreversible.

All the cards are placed face down on the table and each person has to pick up six. They are then allowed to swap one card on each turn.

Hannah, David and Nick have been playing the game, one of them has now won. Here are their cards.

*Hannah's hand*

*Nick's hand*

*David's hand*

● Who is the winner?

The winner is Nick. He is the only person who has the right cards for three matching pairs:

Clay being fired into bricks: Irreversible change
Wood burning on the fire: Irreversible change
Chocolate melting: Reversible change

**1** Fill in the gaps in the following sentence:

Physical changes are usually ..............................................................
and ........................................................ changes are not.

Use the picture above to help you answer questions 2–5.

**2** What type of change has taken place in the boiled eggs?

**3** How is the change in the butter that has been spread on the hot toast different from the change in the egg?

**4** Why can't the burnt toast be changed back into normal bread?

**5** The water vapour coming from the boiling pan turns back into liquid water droplets when it hits a cool surface. What is the scientific word used for this change?

**6** Nathan was looking at a candle burning. The wax was melting and running down the side of the candle but it was also burning on the wick. Give two differences between these changes.

**7** In *Using your knowledge*, look again at Hannah's and David's hands. What 'change' cards did they need to complete their sets?

Answers and Guidance are given on p.42.  **How long did you take?**

🕐 *You should be able to complete these questions in 10 minutes*

1   The plastic bottle has lemonade in it.

   Write in the boxes to show the parts which are:

   | solid |        | liquid |        | gas |

   One has been done for you.

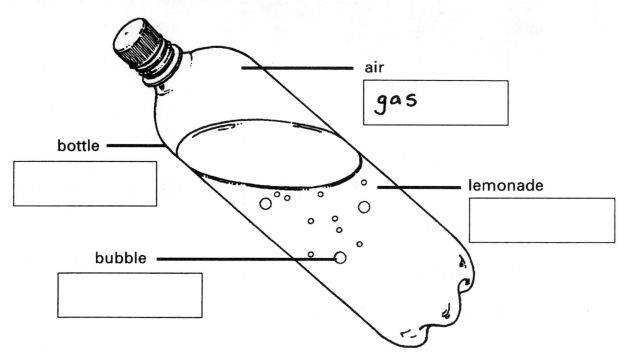

air

gas

bottle

lemonade

bubble

*3 marks*

2

**(a)** Tick **TWO** boxes to show properties that apply to solids but **not** to liquids.

They hold their own shape when you leave them alone. ☐

They will take the shape of the container they are poured into. ☐

Their surface stays level if you tip the container they are in. ☐

They can all be touched and 'got hold of'. ☐

*2 marks*

**(b)** Tick the table to show those changes that are reversible.

| Change | Is this change reversible? |
|---|---|
| Chocolate being gently heated | |
| A candle burning | |
| Orange juice being frozen to make an ice lolly | |
| Wet Plaster of Paris going hard | |

*1 mark*

3

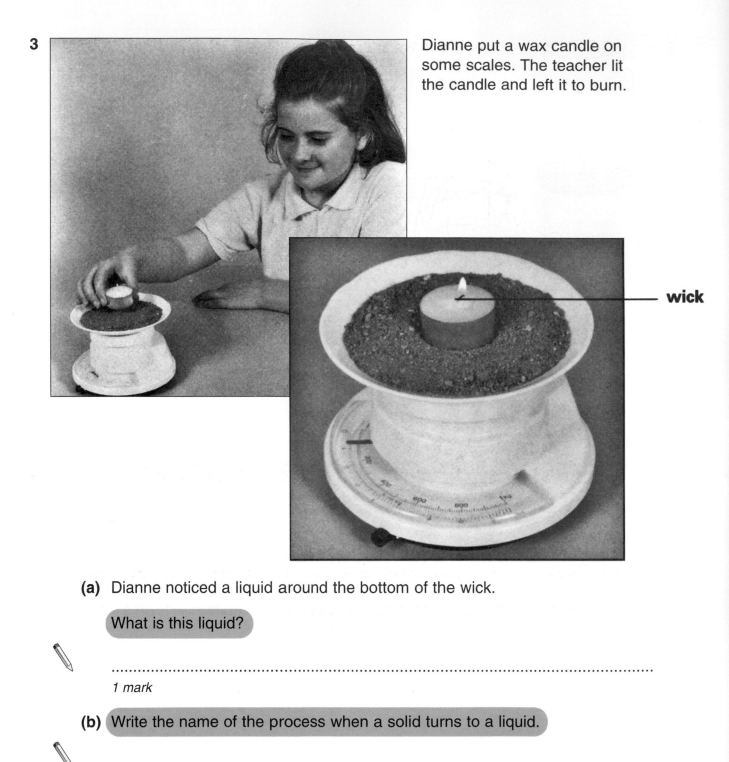

Dianne put a wax candle on some scales. The teacher lit the candle and left it to burn.

wick

(a) Dianne noticed a liquid around the bottom of the wick.

What is this liquid?

..................................................................................................................

*1 mark*

(b) Write the name of the process when a solid turns to a liquid.

..................................................................................................................

*1 mark*

1998 A6

26

(c) Dianne measured the mass of the candle every 30 minutes.

Her results are shown on this graph.

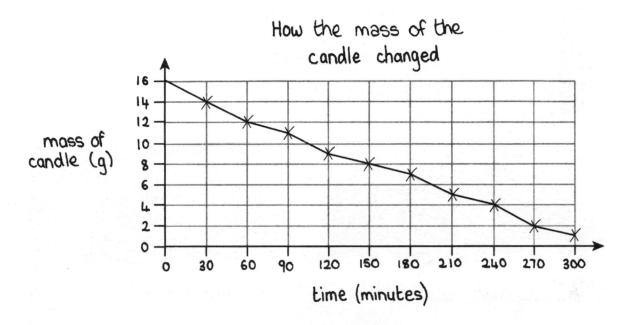

Look at the graph.

What happened to the mass of the candle while it was burning?

..................................................................................................................................................

*1 mark*

(d) Gareth said, 'When the candle wax burns, the change can be reversed.'

Dianne did not agree with him. She said, 'This change is irreversible.'

Explain why Dianne is correct.

..................................................................................................................................................

*1 mark*

1998 A6

Answers and Guidance are given on p.46.    *How long did you take?*

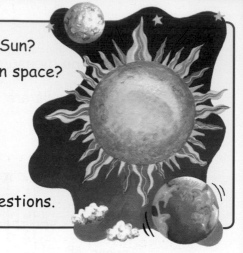

| What you need to know | ★ What shape are the Earth, the Moon and the Sun? |
| --- | --- |

★ What shape are the Earth, the Moon and the Sun?

★ How are the Earth, Moon and Sun positioned in space?

★ How do we get night and day?

★ Why does the Sun appear to move in the sky?

★ What is the orbit of the Earth?

★ Why does the Moon appear to change shape?

This chapter will help you to answer these key questions.

## The Earth, Moon and Sun

The Earth, Moon and Sun are all **spheres**. This means they are shaped like a ball or a globe.

The Sun is by far the biggest of the three, and is a massive ball of burning gas.

The Earth is about seven times bigger than the Moon but much, much smaller than the Sun.

The diagram below shows the positions of the Earth, Moon and the Sun. The pictures are not to scale because the Sun is gigantic compared with the Earth and Moon.

## Night and day

The Earth spins on its **axis** once every 24 hours. The axis is an imaginary line through the centre of the Earth. The Sun does not spin; it stays still in the centre of our solar system.

The part of the Earth that faces the Sun gets light from the Sun, giving us what we call **day**. The part of the Earth that is not lit by the Sun is in darkness and we call this **night**.

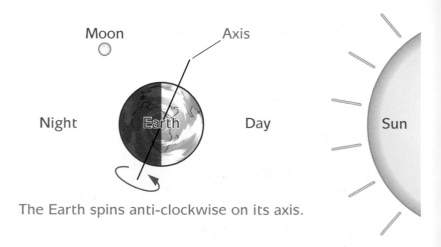

The Earth spins anti-clockwise on its axis.

## Why does the Sun appear to move in the sky?

Imagine there is a girl, Estelle, standing on the model of the Earth in the picture. She is standing at position A. It is the middle of the night and she cannot see the Sun at all.

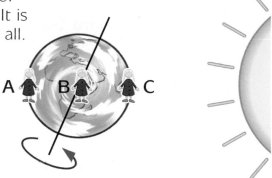

As the Earth continues to spin on its axis, Estelle is gradually moved to position B. Here she is just beginning to see the Sun: it will appear low in the sky on the horizon. This is what we call **sunrise**.

By lunch time Estelle will be standing at position C. The Sun will be overhead, high in the sky.

As the Earth continues to spin, she will gradually be moved around until she can only just see the Sun: it will appear low in the sky. This is what we call **sunset**. After sunset, Estelle will not be able to see the Sun and it will be night once more.

## The orbit of the Earth

As well as spinning on its axis, the Earth goes around the Sun. The scientific way of describing the Earth's path around the Sun is to say the Earth **orbits** the Sun. We say that it takes 365 days for the Earth to orbit the Sun. This is one year in our calendar.

More accurately, it takes the Earth takes $365\frac{1}{4}$ days to orbit the Sun, but to make it easier we have 3 years with 365 days in them. Every fourth year we then have 366 days to account for four $\frac{1}{4}$ days. We call the year with 366 days a **leap year**. In leap years February has a 29th day.

| February | | | | | | |
|---|---|---|---|---|---|---|
| S | M | T | W | T | F | S |
| | | 1 | 2 | 3 | 4 | 5 |
| 6 | 7 | 8 | 9 | 10 | 11 | 12 |
| 13 | 14 | 15 | 16 | 17 | 18 | 19 |
| 20 | 21 | 22 | 23 | 24 | 25 | 26 |
| 27 | 28 | 29 | | | | |

## The shape and orbit of the Moon

The Moon orbits the Earth. It takes about 28 days for the Moon to go once around the Earth.

The Moon is lit by the Sun like the Earth is. We can see the Moon at night because it reflects light from the Sun. It does not give out light itself, it only reflects it from the Sun. Depending on the position of the Earth and the Moon, sometimes only part of the lit side of the Moon can be seen. This is why the Moon appears to change shape.

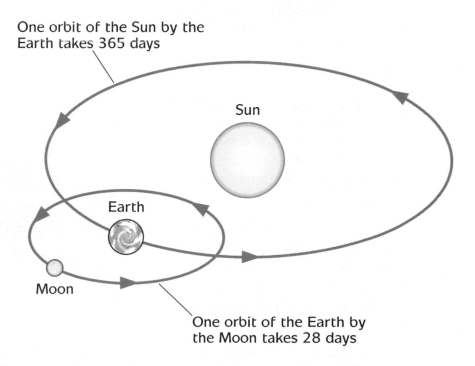

One orbit of the Sun by the Earth takes 365 days

Sun

Earth

Moon

One orbit of the Earth by the Moon takes 28 days

### Why does the Sun appear to move?

Some children decided to track the position of the Sun throughout the day to find out exactly what happens. They got the school caretaker to help because they wanted to record the position of the Sun from early in the morning until late in the afternoon.

They were careful not to stare directly at the Sun, as staring at the Sun can damage your eyes.

The children made a mark on the floor of their classroom. From this position the children then looked to see where the Sun was through the window. They marked this position on the window by drawing a cross with a marker pen. Next to the cross, they also wrote the time at which they looked.

At the end of the afternoon, this is what the window looked like:

The children noticed that the Sun seemed to move in an arc.

● Why did the Sun appear to change position?

During the day the Earth is spinning on its axis. Gradually we are changing our position on Earth compared with the Sun. The Sun remains still. Because we cannot feel the Earth spinning our minds are tricked into thinking it is the Sun that is moving, not us!

If you looked out of the window in the photograph you would be facing south.

● What direction does the Sun rise?

The Sun rises in the east. We know this because the children first marked crosses low down on the left-hand side of the window. This is the east side.

● In what direction does the Sun set?

The Sun sets in the west. By following their arc of crosses and using a compass the children could work out that the Sun had seemed to move towards the west.

**1** Put these in order of size, starting with the smallest.

Earth      Moon      Sun

**2** Which of these features do the Sun, Earth and Moon all have in common? Tick one box.

They are all spinning ☐      They are all in orbit ☐

They are all spheres ☐      They all give off light ☐

**3** The Earth moves in two ways through space.
  **a** Which type of movement causes day and night?
  **b** Which type of movement causes a year?
  **c** Which type of movement causes the Sun to appear to move through the sky?

**4** Match up the following times.

| | |
|---|---|
| Time the Earth takes to go round the Sun | 24 hours |
| Time the Earth takes to spin on its axis | 28 days |
| Time for the Moon to orbit the Earth | 365 days |

**5** Look again at *Using your knowledge*. What would the children need to do to be more accurate about finding the time that the Sun is at its highest point in the sky?

Answers and Guidance are given on p.43.    **How long did you take?**

# 6 Shadows

**What you need to know**

★ What is a shadow?

★ Do all objects make shadows?

★ How can we work out the size of a shadow?

★ How can we make shadows change size?

★ Why do the shadows made by sunlight change size during the day?

This chapter will help you to answer these key questions.

## Shadows

A **shadow** is made when an object blocks light. Light travels in straight lines: it cannot bend round objects. If an object is in the way of a ray of light and the object does not let light through it, then a shadow will be made.

## Making shadows

For a shadow to be made, the object must block the light. Materials that do not let any light through them are called **opaque** materials. We cannot see through opaque materials. Opaque materials make dark shadows that are easily seen.

Some materials let the light through easily. They are called **transparent** materials. We can see through transparent materials. Transparent materials do not block the light so they do not form shadows.

There are some materials that only let a small amount of light through. They are called **translucent** materials. We can just about see through translucent materials. If the light is strong you can get shadows formed because the translucent materials block the light a little. The shadows are often fuzzy and faint.

| Opaque materials | Translucent materials | Transparent materials |
|---|---|---|

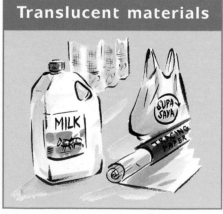

# Drawing the shadows of objects

You can make a shadow using a powerful torch and a cut-out card cat stuck on a stick. The cat puppet blocks the light and a shadow is formed on the screen.

Using a ruler and a pencil, we can draw a diagram to show where the shadow is made and what size it will be.

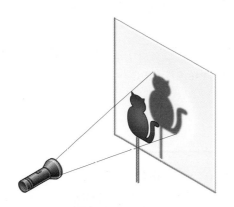

Remember that light travels in straight lines from the source of the light. Light does not curve round objects. Anything that blocks the light will leave a shadow. So if we draw straight lines (representing the light) from the torch to the cat puppet, those that pass the edge of the puppet will form the edge of the shadow on the whiteboard.

# Changing the size of shadows

You can change the size of the shadow by moving the position of the torch. If you bring the torch close to the cat the shadow will get bigger. Look at the diagram on the right. The torch is closer to the cat than in the diagram above and the cat is blocking more of the light.

If you move the torch further away from the cat puppet, the shadow will be smaller.

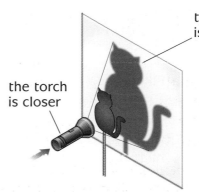

the shadow is bigger

the torch is closer

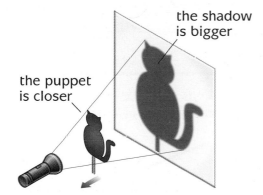

the shadow is bigger

the puppet is closer

You can also change the size of the shadow by keeping the torch still and moving the puppet nearer or further way from the torch. If the puppet and the torch are close together, the shadow is large. If the puppet is moved away from the torch, the shadow will be much smaller.

# Shadows made by sunlight

On a sunny day you will see many shadows. If it is very hot you may sit in the shade of a tree. This shade is the shadow formed by the tree blocking the sunlight. During the day the shadow from the tree will move and change size. This is because the Earth is spinning on its axis and is changing its position in relation to the Sun.

The Sun rises in the east and sets in the west. During the day the Sun appears to move in a great arc across the sky, and is highest around mid-day. Look at the pictures below to see how this causes the shape and position of shadows to change.

*The Sun appears low in the sky in the east. The shadow is long.*

*The Sun is high in the sky, it is around mid-day. The shadow is short.*

*The Sun appears low in the sky in the west. The shadow is long.*

## Using your knowledge

### How does the angle of the torch affect the length of the shadow?

Some children decided to find out whether the angle at which they hold a torch affects the shadow of a model animal. They planned an investigation exploring a range of angles.

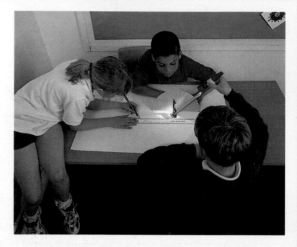

To make it a fair test they kept the model in the same position each time, and kept the torch the same distance from the model. They used a large protractor to help them measure the angle at which they held the torch.

They recorded their results.

To help them find any pattern in their results the children thought they should draw a graph.

● What type of graph should they draw?

| Angle of torch | Length of shadow |
|---|---|
| 20° | 84 cm |
| 40° | 65 cm |
| 60° | 43 cm |
| 80° | 25 cm |

The children can draw a line graph because both the angle of the torch and the length of the shadow are results that are numbers, and the length of shadow changes little by little, not in big jumps. There is more about drawing graphs in Chapter 6 of Book 4.

The points on the graph can be joined up to make a smooth line.

● Can you answer the children's question: 'How does the angle of the torch affect the length of the shadow?'

*A line graph to show the length of the shadow made when a torch is held at different angles*

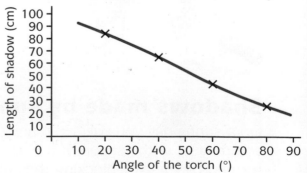

When the torch was at a smaller angle the shadow was longer.
When the torch was held at a larger angle the shadow was shorter.
We can say the greater the angle of the torch the smaller the shadow.

## Test yourself

**1** Here are six different materials: **clear glass**, **wood**, **tracing paper**, **stone**, **iron**, **frosted glass**. Put each one into the correct group below.

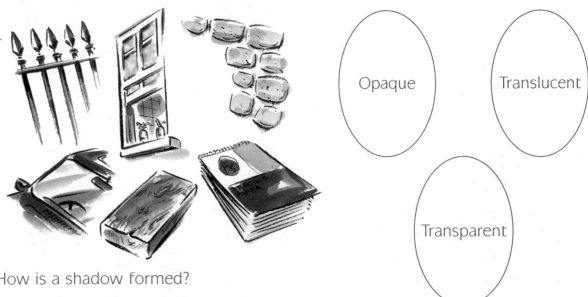

Opaque

Translucent

Transparent

**2** How is a shadow formed?

**3** What types of objects make dark shadows?

**4** What do we call objects that make no shadow at all?

**5** Two children are making animal shadows using a torch and their hands. Maya holds the torch while Nimish makes the animal shapes with his fingers. Fill in the gaps in the sentences below using any of the following words: **away from**, **bigger**, **nearer**, **smaller**. You can use the words more than once.

To make the shadow bigger Maya should move the torch ............................. Nimish's hands. Nimish could also make the shadow bigger by moving his hands ......................... the torch. If Maya moves the torch further away from Nimish the shadow gets ......................... .

**6** Justine notices that the shadow made by an object moves but the object stays still. What must have happened to make the shadow move?

**7** Look again at *Using your knowledge*. Which will make a longer shadow: when the torch is held at 80° or at 40°?

80°     40°

 Answers and Guidance are given on p.44.    ***How long did you take?***

**35**

🕐 *You should be able to complete these questions in 13 minutes*

1   Tim and Sue have a torch and a shadow puppet.

(a)  The height of the puppet is 20 cm.

The graph below shows how the height of the shadow on the screen changed when the puppet was moved away from the torch.

1997 A5

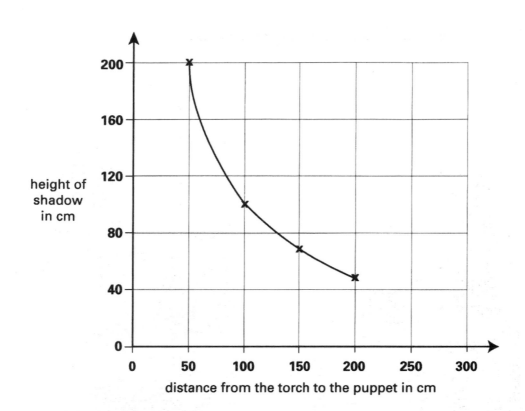

distance from the torch to the puppet in cm

Continue the line graph to show what the height of the shadow will be when the puppet is 250 cm and 300 cm from the torch.

*2 marks*

**(b)** Look at the graph.

What was the height of the shadow when the puppet was 50 cm from the torch?

.......................... cm.

*1 mark*

**(c)** Describe how the height of the shadow changed as the distance from the torch to the puppet changed.

........................................................................................................

*2 marks*

1997 A5

**2** **(a)** The children measured the length of the stick's shadow at different times on a day in summer.

At 9 o'clock in the morning, the Sun is shining.

Explain how the shadow of the stick is formed.

✏ ..................................................................................................................

..................................................................................................................

*1 mark*

**(b)** At 3 o'clock in the afternoon, the Sun appears to be in a different position in the sky.

Explain why the Sun appears to have moved.

✏ ..................................................................................................................

..................................................................................................................

*1 mark*

1998 A7

**38**

**(c)** At 7 o'clock in the evening the Sun appears to have moved further.

Which of the diagrams below shows the position of the shadow at 7 o'clock in the evening?

Tick **ONE** box.

 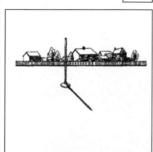  

*1 mark*

**(d)** Debbie measured the length of a shadow at different times during the day. She recorded her results.

| Time | Length of shadow |
|---|---|
| 10 am | 132 cm |
| 11 am | 109 cm |
| 12 noon | 91 cm |
| 1 pm | 80 cm |
| 2 pm | ? |
| 3 pm | 108 cm |

Tick the box below which shows the length of the shadow at 2 p.m.

Tick **ONE** box.

81 cm ☐    90 cm ☐    105 cm ☐    110 cm ☐

*1 mark*

**(e)** Explain why the shadow was shortest at 1 pm.

..........................................................................................................

*1 mark*

1998 A7

3

Complete the following sentences.

The Earth spins on its axis once every ...................................................... hours.

*1 mark*

The half of the Earth facing away from the Sun is in ......................................... .

*1 mark*

It takes about 365 days for the Earth to orbit the ................................................. .

*1 mark*

1997 A1

Answers and Guidance are given on p.46. | *How long did you take?* |

# Answers and Guidance

## 1 Your skeleton and teeth

**1** **The skull protects the brain**.

**2** The three main jobs that the skeleton does are **supports our body**, **helps us move** and **protects our organs**.

**3** a Your **elbow is a hinge joint**.

  b Your **hip is a ball and socket joint**.

Move the joints you are asked about to see how you can move them. Your elbow allows your forearm to move up and down but not side to side. This is the same kind of movement as the knee joint, which you have found out is a hinge joint.

Your hip allows your leg to move from side to side as well as forwards and back. The shoulder joint can also move like this and we know that this joint is a ball and socket joint.

**4**
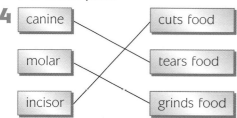

| canine | cuts food |
| molar | tears food |
| incisor | grinds food |

**5** You could have written down any three of the following:

- **brushing your teeth at least twice a day**
- **using dental floss**
- **using mouthwash**
- **visiting the dentist regularly**

You should not have said 'reduce the amount of chocolate or sweets you eat'. This might help you look after your teeth if you did the other things as well, but if you just cut down on chocolate and did nothing else to look after your teeth it would not really help.

**6** **It is important not to leave sugar on your teeth for a long period of time because bacteria feed on the sugar and change it to acid. The bacteria, along with the sugar and acid are called plaque. The acid decays the teeth**.

**7** As well as a large surface area, **the molars have ridges that grind against each other when you chew your food. This helps crush the food**.

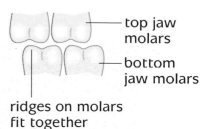

top jaw molars

bottom jaw molars

ridges on molars fit together

*Target time for all questions: 13 minutes*

*Your time for all questions*

## 2 Your heart and blood

**1** **The heart pumps blood around the body**.

**2** **The ribs protect the heart**.

**3** Blood moves away from the heart in blood vessels called **arteries**. It returns to the heart in blood vessels called **veins**.

An easy way to help you remember that the arteries carry blood away from your heart is that **a**rteries and **a**way both start with the letter **a**.

**4** Your pulse rate tells you **how many times your heart beats in a minute**.

It does not tell you anything about your breathing, nor does it tell you about the amount of blood being pumped.

**5** **Your heart beat rate goes up when you do exercise because your body is using up the food and oxygen that is carried in the blood to the muscles. If the muscles are working harder, the heart also has to work harder by beating faster to send more food and oxygen to the muscles**.

**6** **When you stop exercising your pulse rate starts to return to the resting pulse rate.** This can take some time.

**7** Susan's pulse rate will return to its resting rate after about **14 minutes**.

Here is another important use of line graphs. You can extend the line into the unknown! Continue the line graph and you will notice that your line continues to drop in a curved line. Susan's resting pulse rate is 80 beats per minute, so all you need to do is find 80 on the vertical axis. Come straight across from this value to your new line that you have just drawn in. Once

# Answers and Guidance

you hit the line, come down and find out the reading on the time axis. You can see that it is 14 minutes.

*A line graph to show Susan's pulse rate for 12 minutes after exercise.*

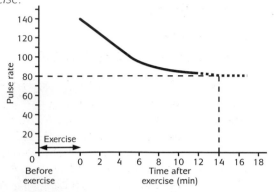

⏱ **Target time for all questions: 11 minutes**

⏱ **Your time for all questions**

## 3 Solids, liquids and gases

**1** Solid: **sand, bottle, plastic bucket, sea shell, deckchair**

Liquid: **suntan lotion, sea, lemonade**

Gas: **bubbles in lemonade, air in balloon**

**2** You could have written any two of the following:

● **Solid butter can be cut or shaped**.

● **Solid butter holds its own shape when left alone**.

● **Solid butter can be got hold of**.

● **Solid butter cannot be poured**.

**3** You could have written any two of the following:

● **Liquid butter can be poured**.

● **Liquid butter will take the shape of the container it is in**.

● **Liquid butter will remain level when the container is tipped**.

● **Liquid butter will flow to the lowest level possible**.

**4** **Most gases are normally invisible whereas you can see liquids**.

You should not have said that gases take the shape of the container they are in, because so do liquids and

you have been asked to give a property that gases and liquids do not share. So, you should not have said that gases will spread out because liquids do this too.

**5** a Solid ——— **Melting** ——→ Liquid

b Gas ——— **Condensation** ——→ Liquid

c Liquid ——— **Evaporation** ——→ Gas

**6** **Sand and sugar can be poured**.

These solids are made of very small grains. Each tiny piece holds its shape but because they are so small together they will 'flow' from one container to another.

**7**

| Substance | Reading on syringe after compression |
|---|---|
| Sand | 5 cm³ |
| Air | 0.5 cm³ |
| Orange juice | 5 cm³ |
| **Iron filings** | 5 cm³ |
| **Fizzy lemonade** | 4.8 cm³ |
| **Water** | 5 cm³ |
| Plasticine | **5 cm³** |

The new substances are all solid or liquid so they cannot be compressed. Fizzy lemonade contains gas bubbles that can be squashed down a little. That is why the children were able to move the syringe in a little.

⏱ **Target time for all questions: 12 minutes**

⏱ **Your time for all questions**

## 4 Changing and changing back

**1** Physical changes are usually **reversible** and **chemical** changes are not.

**2** **An irreversible chemical change has taken place in the boiled eggs**.

You cannot get the raw egg back once you have boiled it because you have changed the chemicals that make up the egg.

**3** **The butter on the hot toast has melted. This change in the butter is a physical change that can be reversed**.

You can get the butter back to its solid form because you have not changed the chemicals, only the state of the substance.

42

# Answers and Guidance

**4** Burnt toast cannot be changed back into normal bread because the chemicals in it have been changed by burning.

**5** The scientific word for the change when water vapour turns back into water droplets is condensation.

This process is a reversible change. The water is still the same substance it has just changed its state.

**6** The wax melting is an example of a physical change that can be reversed. The liquid wax can be cooled and return to the state of solid wax.

The wax burning is an example of an irreversible chemical change. As the wax burns it changes into new substances and gives off heat. The burnt wax cannot be turned back to solid wax.

**7** Hannah needed one card. She needed to swap a reversible change for an irreversible change card.

This would have given her the following pairs:

| | |
|---|---|
| Match burning: | Irreversible change |
| Orange juice freezing to make a lolly: | Reversible change |
| Bread dough being baked into bread: | Irreversible change |

**David needed one card. He needed to swap a reversible change for an irreversible change card.**

This would have given him the following pairs:

| | |
|---|---|
| Candle burning: | Irreversible change |
| Water freezing to make ice cubes: | Reversible change |
| Bread being heated to a high temperature to make toast: | Irreversible change |

 **Target time for all questions: 13 minutes**

 **Your time for all questions**

## 5 The Earth, Moon and Sun

**1** Moon, Earth, Sun

The Moon is the smallest and the Sun the biggest.

**2** You should have ticked **They are all spheres**.

The Sun does not spin. It remains still at the centre of our solar system. The Moon does not spin, it just moves round the Earth keeping one side facing the Earth all the time. The Sun is not in orbit, but the Earth orbits the Sun and the Moon orbits the Earth. The Earth and Moon are solid but the Sun is a giant ball of gases that is a source of light.

**3** a **The Earth rotating or spinning on its axis causes day and night.**

b **The Earth orbiting the Sun takes a year.**

c **The Earth rotating or spinning on its axis causes the Sun to appear to move through the sky.**

Make sure you are clear about these two types of movement, and when you are asked about a type of movement, make sure your answer is clearly talking about just one type of movement.

**4**

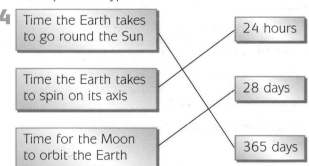

**5** **To be more accurate about finding the time that the Sun was at its highest point in the sky the children would need to take more readings.**

They thought that it was at its highest at 12 o'clock but it could have been higher at 11.50 a.m. or 12.10 p.m. They would need to check at smaller intervals of time, for example 10 or 15 minute intervals, between 11 a.m. and 1.00 p.m.

 **Target time for all questions: 10 minutes**

**Your time for all questions**

**43**

# Answers and Guidance

## 6 Shadows

**1**

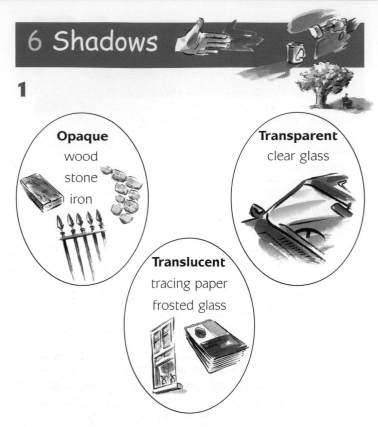

**Opaque**
wood
stone
iron

**Transparent**
clear glass

**Translucent**
tracing paper
frosted glass

**2 Shadows are formed when an object blocks light.**

Light travels in straight lines past the object but there is an area of darkness where the object has stopped the light.

**3 Opaque objects make dark shadows.**

This is because they completely block the light.

**4 Objects that make no shadow at all are transparent.**

In other words they let through all the light.
No light is blocked to form a shadow.

**5** To make the shadow bigger Maya should move the torch **nearer** Nimish's hands. Nimish could also make the shadow bigger by moving his hands **nearer** the torch. If Maya moves the torch further away from Nimish the shadow gets **smaller**.

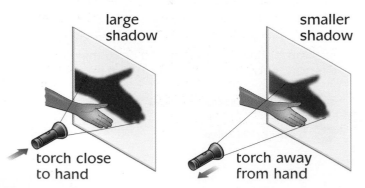

large shadow

smaller shadow

torch close to hand

torch away from hand

**6 If the object has stayed still but its shadow has moved we know that the light source must have moved.**

**7** When the torch is held at an angle of 80°, the shadow will be short as the torch is nearly directly above the model. When the torch is held at an angle of 40°, the shadow will be long.

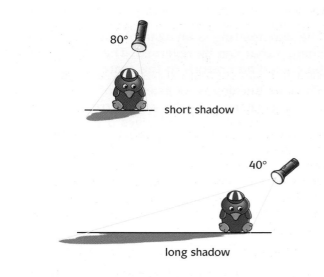

80°

short shadow

40°

long shadow

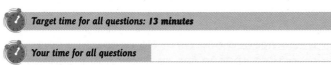

*Target time for all questions: 13 minutes*

*Your time for all questions*

# Answers and Guidance

## National Test Questions 1

**1 a** You would get one mark for one of the following:

- **brush/clean teeth**
- **use floss**
- **use mouthwash**

You would also get the mark if you had said '**chew gum**' but not if you had said 'wash your teeth'. A common mistake in questions like this is to say things like 'eat fruit' or 'don't eat sweets', which is not quite enough. If you ate fruit but never cleaned your teeth you would still get plaque!

**b (i) Molars grind or crush food**.

You would get the mark if you had said '**chews**', '**crunches**' or '**smashes**' food but if you gave a general feature of teeth, like breaks the food into little pieces or bites food, you would not get the mark. Another reason why you would not get the mark for writing 'bites' is that it is information that is already given to you in the question.

**b (ii) Incisors chop, cut or slice food**.

You would get the mark if you had said '**chisel**' or '**nibble**' food, but again if you said a general feature of all teeth, such as 'bite', you would not get the mark.

CROSS-CHECK CHAPTER 1

**2 a contract**

Muscles can only contract and then relax.

**b** (i) and (ii) You could have written any one of the following for each answer (but not the same one for each answer):

- **support**, for example to stand upright, keep a solid shape, and prevent your body collapsing
- **movement**, for example to help you run and swim, to be able to move, because muscles are attached to them
- **protection**, for example to protect organs such as your brain and lungs

You would also get the marks if you said things like '**makes red blood cells**' or '**transmits sound**'.

You are asked for two different ways that the skeleton is important to humans. That means if you give two answers that mean the same thing then you will only get one mark. So for example, if you said 'to help you run' for part (i) and 'to help you swim' for part (ii), you would only get one mark because they are two types of movement. If you said 'to prevent you from collapsing' and 'to keep you a solid shape', again you would get just one mark. You must make sure you give different ways.

Finally, you would get the marks if you answered in the negative, for example if you wrote '**without a skeleton you can't walk**' or '**without a skeleton you'd collapse**' but try to get in the habit of answering the question that was asked. In this case you were asked 'Why is the skeleton important?' not 'What would the problem be if you did not have a skeleton?'

CROSS-CHECK CHAPTER 1

**3 a eating lots of fatty foods** and **smoking** could lead to a greater chance of heart disease.

In these types of questions it is important that you follow the instructions. It says tick TWO boxes. So make sure you put ticks not crosses and make sure you only tick two boxes. If, for example, you ticked three boxes and two of your ticks were correct you would only get one mark because one of the three ticks has to be wrong.

**b The heart pumps blood around the body**.

You would get the mark if you put '**the heart pumps blood**' with no mention of the body. But if you used words like the heart 'sends' or 'pushes' or 'moves' blood you would need to be specific about where, in other words 'round the body'. Another common mistake in questions like this is to be unclear about what you are talking about in the answer by using the word 'it'. For example 'it pumps blood round the body' would get the mark, but 'it pumps it' would not because it would not be clear what was being pumped by what.

**c veins**

**d 78** and **78**

In this question, the examiners would have allowed your answer to be 4 either side of 78 (in other words from 74 to 82). The science is about the resting pulse rate being the same after resting for a long period of time after exercise. Whatever exercise Mary does, her pulse will eventually return to the same resting pulse rate.

**e After resting the heart beat rate returns to its resting rate**.

You would have got the mark if you said pulse rate rather than heart beat rate, and you would also get the mark if you said it returned to normal after resting. You would not get the mark if you did not mention the pulse or heart, for example if you said 'because she rested', 'they are all the same' or 'it is always 78' you would not get the mark.

CROSS-CHECK CHAPTER 2

# Answers and Guidance

## National Test Questions 2

**1** You would get one mark each for:

bottle: **solid**

lemonade: **liquid**

bubble: **gas**

CROSS-CHECK CHAPTER 3

**2** a   The two properties that apply to solids but not to liquids are:

● **They hold their own shape when you leave them alone**.

● **They can all be touched and 'got hold of'**.

b   You should have ticked **Chocolate being gently heated** and **Orange juice being frozen to make an ice lolly**. The other two reactions are irreversible because they involve chemical changes and new substances are formed.

CROSS-CHECK CHAPTER 4

**3** a   **Melted wax** or **liquid wax**.

You would get the mark if you said melted candle, but you would not the mark if you just wrote 'candle' by itself.

b   The process is **melting**.

You would get the mark if you said '**melts**' but not if you said 'turns to liquid', 'liquefies' or 'liquidised' as these words could also describe condensation, when a gas cools to make a liquid. You would not get the mark for answers like 'warming up', which does not describe the change of state, or 'thaws', which is a term that only really applies to solid ice turning to water.

c   **The mass of the candle decreased or got smaller**.

You would get the mark if you put 'it went down', 'it got lower or less', 'it got lighter' or 'the weight dropped'. If you gave the impression that you did not read the graph but just talked about the candle getting shorter or melting away then you would not get the mark.

d   **The change cannot be reversed because burning is a chemical change and new chemicals are made**.

If you wrote that you cannot get the wax back, or that it had changed into a different material, then you would get the mark. If you wrote that the wax disappears or that the wax turns to gas then you were not being specific enough. The most common mistake with this question is to confuse things by talking about wax melting. This, of course, is a physical change and can be reversed. You need to indicate that burning is a chemical change.

CROSS-CHECK CHAPTER 4

## National Test Questions 3

**1** a   You would get one mark for continuing your line to the **300 cm** distance mark. You would get one mark for ending up between the **20 and 40 cm height marks**.

How do you work out how to continue the line? You have to continue the drawn curve to the 300 mark because that is what you are told to do. You know the line is going to continue to fall so it will go below 40 cm, but it cannot go below 20 cm because that is the height of the puppet. Shadows are never smaller than the object blocking the light. Your answer can be either of the two lines drawn on the graph below, or anywhere within the shaded area.

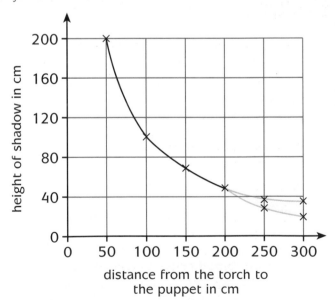

b   **200**

This is a straightforward bit of graph reading, so you must get it exactly right to get the mark. You would lose the mark if you wrote down some units other than cm, because cm is printed for you.

# Answers and Guidance

c **The nearer the puppet to the torch the larger the shadow** or **the further the puppet from the torch the smaller the shadow**.

This answer is worth two marks. You would get the two marks if you talked about the distance of the puppet from the screen, for example the further the puppet from the screen the larger the shadow, but why live dangerously? You were asked about the distance from the torch and the height of puppet, so stick to that.

We will be doing a lot more about these types of questions throughout *Success in Science*, especially in Chapter 6 of Book 4. It is important that you describe a general pattern that links together all the results. A common mistake is just to talk about one or two pairs of results, for example, 'the furthest one is the shortest and the nearest is the tallest'. These types of answers only get half the marks when your test papers are marked because they do not talk about all the results on the graph.

You would score no marks if you talked about things other than height and distance, for example 'the closer the puppet is, the darker it is', or if you tried to explain what is going on rather than describing the results, for example 'the closer it is, the more light it blocks'. Finally watch the language you use and be precise. If, for example, you put 'as it gets closer, it gets bigger' you have used the word 'it' once too often for your answer to be clear.

**CROSS-CHECK** CHAPTER 6

**2** a **A shadow is caused because the stick blocks the light**.

It really is worth learning this answer. You will get the mark so long as you talk about light and blocking. **'The Sun's rays are blocked'**, **'the stick is opaque'**, **'the sunlight can't pass through'** and **'the stick does not let the sunlight through'** are all correct answers.

There are three common mistakes on questions about shadows. The first is to give a description of the shadow rather than an explanation, for example 'a shadow is a place where there is no light' or ' a shadow is a dark patch behind the stick' would not get a mark. The second is to give correct information that is not really relevant, for example 'light travels in straight lines' or 'light can't bend past the stick' are correct facts, but they do not answer the question. The third is to use language that is not precise, for example 'light cannot get past the stick' does not tell us about the shadow. There is plenty of light getting past the stick to give us the area of light on the ground, the only light that cannot get past is being blocked by the stick.

b **The Earth has rotated**.

Other acceptable ways of describing this movement are **'the Earth has turned on its axis'** or **'the Earth has spun'**. Unacceptable ways are 'the Earth orbits the Sun' (this gives us a year) and 'the Earth moves' (this is not precise enough). If you had given both movements of the Earth in your answer, for example 'the Earth spins and goes round the Sun', you would not get the mark because you are not being clear about what causes the apparent movement of the Sun.

c You should have ticked the **first box**.

Even if you could not remember the way the Sun appears to move across the sky, you are given all the information you need in the question. In the big picture you are given the shadow for 9 o'clock in the morning. The Sun is on the left of the picture and the shadow comes out to the right. So in the evening the Sun will have apparently moved to the right of the picture and the shadow must come out to the left of the picture. 7 o'clock is just before sunset, so the shadow will point clearly towards the left of the picture. In the fourth picture it is not as far round to the left, so this is not the correct one either.

d **90 cm**

The shadow for 2 pm is going to be approximately half way between the 1 and 3 pm shadows in size.

e **The shadow is shortest because the Sun is at its highest point**.

A common mistake in this type of question is to use unclear language to describe what you mean. For example, if you wrote 'the Sun was high', the Sun might well have been high at 12 and 2 o'clock as well. If you wrote 'the Sun was shining straight down' you might get the mark, but if it was shining straight down there would actually be no shadow. Finally, if you wrote 'the Sun was higher', the meaning is not clear because the examiner will wonder 'higher than what?'

**CROSS-CHECK** CHAPTER 6

# Answers and Guidance

**3** The Earth spins on its axis once every **24** hours

You would get the mark if you said just under 24 hours because the accepted figure for a rotation of the Earth is 23 hours, 56 minutes and 4.09 seconds! Notice that the units for time are printed on the page. If you use another unit you would lose the mark. So do not write things like one day even if you do cross out the 'hours'. It just makes things complicated for the person who marks your test.

The half of the Earth facing away from the Sun is in **darkness**.

You would get the mark if you had written '**the dark**', '**night**' or '**night time**' or even shadow or shade. You are allowed this choice of words because you have to think of your own word or words to complete the sentence. Remember, when you are given a list of words to use make sure you use them.

It takes about 365 days for the Earth to orbit the **Sun**.

You would get the mark if you said '**our star**' but not if you had been less specific and just said 'star'.

CROSS-CHECK CHAPTER 5